Blessed Assurance

Blessed Assurance
Finding Refuge in the Father

Brittany Wilson

Unless otherwise marked, Scripture quotations are taken from the KING JAMES VERSION (KJV): KING JAMES VERSION, public domain.

Scripture quotations marked NIV are taken from the Holy Bible, NEW INTERNATIONAL VERSION®, NIV® Copyright © 1973, 1978, 1984, 2011 by Biblica, Inc.® Used by permission. All rights reserved worldwide.

Scripture quotations marked (NLT) are taken from the Holy Bible, New Living Translation, copyright ©1996, 2004, 2015 by Tyndale House Foundation. Used by permission of Tyndale House Publishers, Inc., Carol Stream, Illinois 60188. All rights reserved.

ISBN: 978-0-9987325-0-3

To my mother and father, who always believe in me.

To my sister, who has been a strong support throughout my life.

And to my Aunt Kathy, who, though I never met her, I know had a wonderful gift for writing. She is one of my biggest inspirations.

Contents

1. Who Is God?
He *Is* Love 12
Blessed Redeemer 14
He Calls Us *Friend* 16
Our Father 18
He Satisfies. 20
The Holy One 22
Loving Discipline 24
The Great Creator. 26
Our Healer. 28
God of Hope 30
Everywhere We Look 32

2. Who Are We in God's Eyes?
He Sees Us. 36
Beautiful as We Are 38
Made to Be You, Made to Be Me 40
Worth the World 42
Forgiven 44
Useful. 46
Understood. 48
Made with a Purpose 50
Gifted for His Glory 52

3. Living for God
Letting Go of "Me" 56
He Is Enough. 58
Grounded in His Word. 60
Look to Him 62
True Repentance. 64
It Starts with a Spark 66
We Will Hear When We Listen. 68

Just Speak.............................70
"Your Will Be Done" 72
Ever Thankful 74
There Is No Compromise.................76
Designed to Thrive 78
Reset..................................80

4. In the Valleys
Fighting the Good Fight 84
Praise Him in the Storm.................86
Spirit Versus Flesh.....................88
The "Perfect" Exchange 90
Living Fearlessly 92
Cast Away Worries 94
Dismissing Doubt 96
Crushing the Night 98
Constant in the Change 102
Desert Dry 104

5. Doing unto Others
Willing to Serve.......................108
Be Their Voice.........................110
Love Is Greatest.......................112
A Heart That Forgives 114
Share the Burden.......................116
Sonnets or Swords?.....................118
Pass It On.............................120
Even the Tiniest Ray...................122
Be Bold................................124

Blessed Assurance. This is not just the title of my book but also my hope for everyone who reads it. I have lived through many trials, disabilities, and illnesses, but God has given me much joy through each one. This joy that comes from knowing Him likewise brings a peace that nothing on earth can provide. I want you, too, to know and experience this.

Within these pages you will find Scripture as well as my own writings on various topics, and they all come back to the same thing: living for Christ. I gave my life to Jesus at seventeen, and while the Christian life isn't free of trouble, it is ever filled with the assurance that God is always by our side through all things.

This book is a reminder of His guarantees. I'll share what Christ promises us: Forgiveness, freedom, love, protection, and so much more. I hope you will see not only the benefits of serving God but gain ideas on how to do so as well.

I hope these writings can be a comfort in whatever hardships you may be facing, and that they will give you blessed assurance that you are, always, in God's hands. I hope, also, that if you don't know Him, through this book you might begin a friendship with Him, surrendering your heart and your life to His will. It is my sincerest wish that He will speak to you and draw you ever closer in your walk with Him.

YOURS IN CHRIST,
Brittany Wilson

1

Who Is God?

He *Is* Love

*God demonstrates his love toward us in this:
while we were still sinners, Christ died for us.*
—ROMANS 5:8 (NIV)

*I am persuaded, that neither death, nor life,
nor angels, nor principalities, nor powers,
nor things present, nor things to come, nor
height, nor depth, nor any other creature,
shall be able to separate us from the love of
God, which is in Christ Jesus our Lord.*
—ROMANS 8:38–39

THROUGHOUT MY LIFE I have been loved by so many: my parents, my friends, my church family. Their love has helped me to endure the many trials life has thrown in my path. Above all, though, there is one love holding me up more than anything else: the love of my God.

Do you ever just sit back and think about the *remarkableness* of God's love? His Word says that His love is so mighty that nothing and no one can separate us from it. He loves us so much that when we were isolated from Him in sin, He sent His own

Son to die in our place so that our sin could be forgiven, allowing us to come into His presence once more.

In His love He also shows us incomparable mercy. As sinners, having chosen our sin over Christ's righteousness, we deserved death, to be separated from Him eternally. Instead, He made a way for us to escape that sentence, at His cost, allowing us to be purified through the blood of His own Son. He promises that if we accept His gift of salvation—place our faith in Him and truly repent—He will welcome us to himself with open arms.

He loves us no matter who we are, and no matter what we have done. We don't have to earn His love and we never could. He offers it to us freely. All we have to do is accept it.

How amazing: In all our wickedness, all our shame, He loves us and nothing can change that. Let us never forget His amazing love. If you've never yet known it, accept His love today, and you'll experience how wonderful and powerful it can be.

Blessed Redeemer

> *Praise be to the God and Father of our Lord Jesus Christ! In His great mercy he has given us new birth into a living hope through the resurrection of Jesus Christ from the dead.*
> —1 Peter 1:3 (NIV)

> *He has rescued us from the dominion of darkness and brought us into the kingdom of the Son he loves, in whom we have redemption, the forgiveness of sins.*
> —Colossians 1:13–14 (NIV)

I AM SO GRATEFUL for what God has done for me. I didn't have any way across the canyon that my sin had placed between God and me. But Jesus paid my price.

Even so, I sometimes lose sight of what this means. When I fall short again and again, I find myself wondering: *How can I love the Lord and yet still make decisions that don't glorify Him?* When this happens, I think, *I must try to do better, to prove myself worthy to Him—worthy of Him.*

In doing this, I am trying to redeem myself; to justify myself. This is something I cannot do.

But that's not a bad thing. In fact, it's glorious. I don't *need* to do this, and neither do you! Furthermore, we already are justified—already redeemed—when we place our faith in Him and ask Him to reside in our hearts, inviting His Spirit to live His perfect life in and through us.

Once we belong to God, we're meant to start a process of being purified, of being made more and more like Jesus every day, in every way. Yet we don't need to be re-justified, or re-redeemed, when we fail. If we do miss the mark, then we turn to the Lord to confess and repent, accept His forgiveness, and move forward.

The main point is, He does the forgiving and the cleansing, just as He did the saving. He's not asking us to prove we're good enough, to show Him that we deserve Him—He only wants us to rely on Him, and live in trusting faith. Salvation is ours if we only ask and believe—it's His gift to us.

We can't be worthy of redemption; rather, it's redemption that makes us right with God and marks us as His children. We can't work for it. Instead, with grateful thanks, we welcome it, and rejoice.

He Calls Us *Friend*

*Take my yoke upon you, and learn of me;
for I am meek and lowly in heart: and
ye shall find rest unto your souls. For my
yoke is easy, and my burden is light.*
—MATTHEW 11:29–30

*Henceforth I call you not servants; for the servant
knoweth not what his lord doeth: but I have
called you friends; for all things that I have heard
of my Father I have made known unto you.*
—JOHN 15:15

THROUGHOUT MY LIFE I have struggled with sin, choosing what I think is best over what God says is better. It has many times harassed and overwhelmed me, bounding me up to the point where I felt the chains might suffocate me. It has tormented and weighed on me until I was knocked flat, leaving me feeling alone and helpless. Before I had Christ, sin made my life a prison, and even as I tried to do good and break free, I would fall back into the enticement of the world, causing the chains to draw even tighter.

That's not to suggest I'm alone in this predicament. The Bible tells us we all come into the world enslaved by sin, by the things of the flesh. We want to do what feels good and ignore what God says is right. His Word says we all have sinned and fallen short of His glory.

Without God, we don't have a choice about this: sin would always have a hold on us.

Fortunately, we don't have to stay that way because God offers us a way out. He saw our suffering, and it saddened Him so much He sent His only Son to die for us.

Jesus bought us with His own blood. This means we belong to God. He owns us.

But you know what? He doesn't treat us as slaves, like Satan does. He calls us *friend*! He doesn't force us to bend to His will—He gives us a choice. He wants us to follow Him, but freely, because we love Him. He wants a relationship with us, for us to know Him, and to experience the fulfillment we can have by the plans He has for us.

When Jesus was here on earth, He didn't walk around with head held high, forcing everyone to bow before Him. He acted as our equal, befriending and serving others and never flaunting His status as God's Son. He doesn't see us as subjects—He sees us as companions, as loved ones He wants to talk with, hear from, and grow closer to.

Isn't it wonderful that the God of the universe, the God who created us, wants not to lord over us but to be our *friend*?

Our Father

See what great love the Father has lavished on us, that we should be called children of God!
—1 John 3:1 (NIV)

I WAS BLESSED TO have parents who have supported me all my life and did everything in their power to give me a good upbringing: showing me the love of Christ, taking care of all of my needs, disciplining me, standing beside me through every trial. They have been there since the beginning, and they know me inside and out.

As caring as they are, however, I have a Father in heaven who is even more wonderful. One who loves me no matter what and who gave everything for me. He not only knows what's best for me, He also already knows exactly what my life holds in store. And he's not just MY Father. God calls all who follow Him His children.

As His children, God knows us completely. His Word says He knew everything about us even before we were born! He knew us as we were being formed in the womb, and even then He already knew how our lives would take shape.

Think about that. Because He knows us so perfectly, He knows perfectly how to help us accomplish His plan for our lives. He is the perfect Father because He already knows our every problem, every need, every step without us having to say anything.

Isn't this astounding? As much as my parents love me, I know God loves me so much more.

Can you call God your Father? He is waiting to welcome you with open arms, to call you His child and help you live the life He's planned just for you.

He Satisfies

*He satisfieth the longing soul, and filleth
the hungry soul with goodness.*
—Psalm 107:9

*Jesus said unto them, I am the bread of life:
he that cometh to me shall never hunger; and
he that believeth on me shall never thirst.*
—John 6:35

One of my favorite contemporary Christian songs, Holly Starr's "Satisfied," is about the satisfaction only God can bring to us. She speaks of how the world tries to make us think it can give us what we need, that it can be enough.

The lyrics make me think of my love for material things. So often I try to find fulfillment in what the world says is good. I try to get the latest clothes; I obsess over singers and actors I find attractive. I think to myself, *I'll be happy if I get the newest gadget* or *if I get into the latest TV show*. But all this stuff just gives me happiness for a short time. It isn't true joy. It doesn't last.

God says we're to look to Him for fulfillment of our desires, because nothing the world has to give can complete us as He can. When we let go of the world and look toward Him, He promises us peace unlike anything the world can provide because true joy and purpose are found only in Him. These are immeasurably better than any short-lived pleasure the world has to offer.

With God we don't have to wander around searching for something to complete us because He does this, always. Worldly happiness is fleeting; the satisfaction God gives is everlasting.

Think about the best day you've ever had, and multiply that by infinity. *That's* what He has in store for us! Instead of looking to the world to find contentment, let's look up.

The Holy One

*Who is like unto thee, O Lord, among the
gods? who is like thee, glorious in holiness,
fearful in praises, doing wonders?*
—Exodus 15:11

*There is none holy as the Lord: for there is none
beside thee: neither is there any rock like our God.*
—1 Samuel 2:2

As a follower of Christ, I think a lot about God's goodness and grace. Yet I often overlook that His Word makes clear that He is a holy God. It is hard to contemplate, let alone truly understand and accept, that because He is perfectly righteous, sin cannot remain in His presence.

God sent His Son to cleanse us of our sins so that we could experience true freedom and live in a relationship with Him. Sometimes, though, even His children can fall back into sinful habits, doing things we know are wrong or filling our minds with thoughts that don't glorify Him. Because He cannot overlook sin, these choices put a wedge between Him and us.

Choosing sin keeps us from having a deeper connection with Him. It keeps us from hearing

His voice and blocks our hearts from the continual renewal of His Spirit. When I experience this myself, I feel far from God, as if my sin is keeping me from getting closer. I get so lost in my sin that I feel numb to God's Word and His presence. In my sin I am keeping Him from helping me become the person He wants me to be.

Thankfully, this can be fixed. He can get rid of that wedge. When we take our sins to God and repent, His Son's sacrifice purifies us, cleanses us, and brings us close to Him again.

If you're indulging in sin, creating a block between you and God, pray today and repent. Ask Him to help you remove that wedge, and invite Him to create a stronger foundation in your life.

Loving Discipline

The word of God is quick, and powerful, and sharper than any twoedged sword, piercing even to the dividing asunder of soul and spirit, and of the joints and marrow, and is a discerner of the thoughts and intents of the heart.
—HEBREWS 4:12

My son, despise not the chastening of the Lord; neither be weary of his correction: For whom the Lord loveth he correcteth; even as a father the son in whom he delighteth.
—PROVERBS 3:11–12

As A GIRL there were many times I was scolded and disciplined in some way. At the time this was not fun, but now that I'm older I can understand that my parents responded as they did to teach me the right way to go. Their correction taught me that there are consequences for doing what's wrong and benefits for doing what's right.

God, like our parents, disciplines His children. I'm reminded of how He dealt with the Israelites' disobedience in the wilderness after He led them out of Egypt. We may read those stories and wonder how a loving God could do something such as make them wander for decades. We may also wonder about the ways He disciplines us in our own lives.

Above all, we can trust that He knows what's best for us, and though we may not fully understand this right away, His discipline will prove it true. Wandering the wilderness, the Israelites had time to contemplate God's goodness and opportunity to come to terms with the ways in which they had sinned against Him.

He disciplines us specifically in accordance with what we have done, and He knows exactly how to help us back on the right path. It's His way of whittling away the bad in our lives and helping us become more like Him. His discipline shows us just how much He loves us. Instead of complaining, let's rejoice in having a God who loves us so much He is willing to do what it takes to keep us from being conquered by the evils of this world.

The Great Creator

When I consider your heavens, the work of your fingers, the moon and the stars, which you have set in place, what is mankind that you are mindful of them, human beings that you care for them? You have made them a little lower than the angels, and crowned them with glory and honor.
—PSALM 8:3–5 (NIV)

By him [Jesus Christ] were all things created, that are in heaven, and that are in earth, visible and invisible, whether they be thrones, or dominions, or principalities, or powers: all things were created by him, and for him.
—COLOSSIANS 1:16

IT TRULY AMAZES me how intricately and beautifully made the earth and its inhabitants are.

Ever since I was a little girl my favorite place has been the beach. Just taking in the view allows me to experience the works of, and ponder the nature of, our awesome Creator. It is so fascinating that God could create something as stunning and dangerous as the sea, with its millions of intricate animals and detailed little shells, worn by the waters over time. All are so different, and each is unique in its own way.

He did the same thing with us, on an even higher level: He created us in His own image. Not only are we each distinctly made, we are designed ingeniously, with multiple systems and parts that work together in harmonious precision to keep us alive and healthy. Think of it! The God who created all that exists—not only the earth but the whole universe and even time—formed us as well.

He made humankind to be perfect, and though because of sin we aren't perfect now, He isn't done with us yet. If we allow Him to continue His work in us, He will keep creating and shaping, with impacts and results beyond our wildest dreams.

Our Healer

*He healeth the broken in heart, and
bindeth up their wounds.*
—Psalm 147:3

*I will restore health unto thee, and I will
heal thee of thy wounds, saith the Lord.*
—Jeremiah 30:17

Year by year, challenge after challenge, I've been given opportunities to learn much about God's healing power.

This has been especially true regarding various illnesses endured by members of my family. And the common theme has been that though they weren't all healed in a way we wanted, they *were* healed.

My grandfather, in his late fifties, suffered through esophageal cancer. We prayed and prayed for healing, for his life on earth to be extended. God chose to heal him by taking him home to heaven.

My mom, while much younger, faced kidney cancer. We prayed and prayed then, too. God chose to heal her by taking the cancer from her body. It never returned.

I don't know why God chose to let my mom

remain longer on earth and decided to bring my grandfather into His presence. What I do know is that He healed them both, and that both healings were miraculous. How could everlasting life in heaven be less miraculous than additional years of life here on earth?

Again, God does not always heal in the way we want, or think we want. However, He certainly knows the kind of healing we need better than we ever could.

This doesn't just apply to physical sickness. It's true in every single facet of our existence, whenever and wherever we need God's divine, supernatural touch. We can always rely on His healing us in the way He knows is best.

And do you know the best thing? Unlike human doctors, the Great Physician never makes a mistake. He is the Lord, our Healer, and His healing is perfect.

God of Hope

*Thou, O Lord, art a shield for me; my
glory, and the lifter up of mine head. I
cried unto the Lord with my voice, and
he heard me out of his holy hill.*
—PSALM 3:3–4

*O death, where is thy sting? O grave, where is thy
victory? The sting of death is sin; and the strength
of sin is the law. But thanks be to God, which
giveth us the victory through our Lord Jesus Christ.*
—1 CORINTHIANS 15:55–57

THERE HAVE BEEN times in my life when I felt so lacking in strength that I could not go any further. I felt pinned under boulders of hurt and God seemed nowhere to be found. It seemed the desert held no water; even the air was as dry as sand, and I heard no answers as I called out for help.

However, even when pain kept me from seeing clearly, always, in the back of my mind, I knew I would hear my Father's voice: "My child, I am here." He has helped me through so much, in so many ways, more times than I can count. He will never leave me, and while I don't always feel this, I forever will believe and know it.

He guarantees that He will always provide what we need, that He will stay beside us through all things, and that we will be with Him through all eternity. He is faithful in all His promises. And so He is our hope—our only hope.

No matter what may bring us low, He can lift us up. Because of what His Son did on the cross for us, we have hope even in the face of death! Because of His work on our behalf, nothing can truly harm us, and evil cannot conquer us.

This is hope in its truest sense—that of assurance, of certainty. Do you have this hope? It is the birthright of all who believe in Him, who belong to Him. You can ask Him, today, to show you how to live assured in Him.

Everywhere We Look

*The eyes of the Lord are in every place,
beholding the evil and the good.*
—PROVERBS 15:3

*Where can I go from your Spirit? Where can I flee
from your presence? If I go up to the heavens, you
are there; if I make my bed in the depths, you are
there. If I rise on the wings of the dawn, if I settle
on the far side of the sea, even there your hand
will guide me, your right hand will hold me fast.*
—PSALM 139:7–10 (NIV)

SOMETIMES I FIND myself feeling alone. God seems far, far away, and I feel disconnected, as if separated from His guidance, protection, and love. It feels like I've been left to fend for myself.

But then I look around. As I slow down and allow myself to breathe, I begin to see Him. I'm reminded of His Word and of what He has done for me in the past.

No matter where I am, I see Him. I see Him in the sunlight, in the breeze, in the flowers. All around us, wherever we look, His creation reflects Him. The sun above gives us life, reminding us each day that He is our Source—our light, our energy, our very air.

In the fall, when the earth is dying, getting ready again to be made new, I think of how God renews us. As snow blankets the earth in winter, I think of the blood of Jesus covering us and washing away our sin. In the spring, flowers and trees bloom once more, reminding me of the new fruit God produces in us; the summer sun reminds me of how His light gives us joy and strength.

God is everywhere we look. Most vitally, His Holy Spirit is in our hearts. Always remember that because of this, no matter what we do or where we go, He will be there, and He will never leave us.

It's important that we take regular, consistent time to look around at, and take note of, what He has created. That we listen to our heart to feel and to hear His Spirit. And that we trust He will—in His way—speak to us, and share himself with us. Wherever we are, wherever we go, He will reveal himself and we'll be reminded of His presence, and His promise: "I am here; I am with you, always."

2

WHO ARE WE IN GOD'S EYES?

He Sees Us

She gave this name to the Lord who spoke to her: "You are the God who sees me," for she said, "I have now seen the One who sees me.
—GENESIS 16:13 (NIV)

I REMEMBER LEARNING ABOUT Greek mythology in high school. The Greek gods were always thinking only of themselves. They never took notice of their supposed creation unless it was to use it for their own selfish ambitions. They didn't care to help others. They only wanted to make sure they themselves were happy.

This makes me so thankful for the one true God, because unlike those false ones, He sees us, and He shows that He cares. Though the universe is so vast and there are so many of us, He sees each of us, and not only that, He also sees inside us and knows who we truly are. We can never hide from Him.

No matter how lost or alone I feel, He will always bring me into His arms. He lets me know that He is aware of what I am going through, that it matters to Him, and that He will never abandon me.

He will do the same for you too. He sees

everything we are, and—even better—He sees everything He can help us to be. Isn't it wonderful to know that the God who made the universe and all of creation sees, knows, and cares for you and me?

Beautiful As We Are

*The Lord said unto Samuel, Look not on his
countenance, or on the height of his stature;
because I have refused him: for the Lord seeth not
as man seeth; for man looketh on the outward
appearance, but the Lord looketh on the heart.*
—1 SAMUEL 16:7

Do you ever think about how we humans view ourselves? Years ago I put my thoughts on this into a poem:

> Looking in the mirror
> What do you see?
> Who you really are
> Or a distorted reality?
>
> Like a funhouse mirror
> Looking much different than it stands
> You stare at the picture in horror
> You cover your eyes with your hands.
>
> Lost in a maze of reflections
> Not knowing where to go
> Confused by what you deem perfection
> Ignoring what you really know.

These words were inspired by the idea that we see ourselves imperfectly. When we look in the mirror, we see blemishes, flaws, fat, or other defects we view as faults that make us undesirable or unworthy.

The fact is that visual reflections don't show the real us. They only show the physical, the outer traits that the world rates highest. The most important aspects, the ones we should be noticing, are what God sees: our personality, our gifts, the distinctive abilities He gave us.

We can see our true selves only with God's eyes. He sees us as we truly are, as He himself designed us, filled with potential. Where we see blemishes, He sees beauty marks, features that make us unique—things He can use for His glory.

Next time you look in the mirror, remember how God sees you, beautiful just the way you are.

Made to Be You, Made to Be Me

> *I will praise thee; for I am fearfully and wonderfully made: marvellous are thy works; and that my soul knoweth right well.*
> —Psalm 139:14

> *Before I formed thee in the belly I knew thee; and before thou camest forth out of the womb I sanctified thee, and I ordained thee a prophet unto the nations.*
> —Jeremiah 1:5

It's evident that each of us is unique in our own way. In general we see this as something positive, but sometimes we may feel we're *too* different. Growing up, I wasn't interested in the same things as my friends. I was always the geeky girl; I was the only one among my friends who loved fantasy and sci-fi. Not only that, I was diagnosed with autism spectrum disorder as well as ADHD. I was never what many might think of as "normal."

What I've come to learn though is that *different* is a good thing. If we were all the same, with identical mannerisms, habits, and hobbies, the world would be extremely boring. It was God who made us one of a kind—each with our own desires, interests, and purposes. Because He designed us in this manner, we all have different ways we can serve Him and others.

Jesus is the ultimate example of being unique in God. He certainly didn't conform to worldly norms. He lived as His father taught Him, even when His actions didn't fit in with society's expectations. He refused to stick to the manmade traditions of the Jews, instead befriending those whom others saw as unclean or unworthy. Whether people followed Him or scoffed at Him, He did what He knew to be right, walking the path God made for Him.

God wants the same thing for us. He wants His children to stand out, to be special in Him so that the world can see His greatness. "Normal" is a human notion that can keep us from going outside societal boundaries and reaching our full potential for Christ. Instead of conforming to the norm, let us reach beyond the usual to be the exceptional people God created us to be.

Worth the World

> *Are not five sparrows sold for two farthings,
> and not one of them is forgotten before
> God? But even the very hairs of your head
> are all numbered. Fear not therefore: ye
> are of more value than many sparrows.*
> —LUKE 12:6–7

> *God so loved the world, that he gave his only
> begotten Son, that whosoever believeth in him
> should not perish, but have everlasting life.*
> —JOHN 3:16

THROUGHOUT MANY BOUTS with depression, I've thought repeatedly about *worth*. What is my worth? What does it mean to have a healthy self-worth? And I wonder how, in the midst of turmoil, so broken myself, I can be of any worth to others.

I've found that the best question to ask is *What am I worth to God?* This gives me the answer that puts everything else in place. I'm worth so much to Him that He sent His own Son to die so that I would belong to Him and enjoy a connection with Him. I'm worth so much that He works in my life to mold me into the likeness of Christ, that He has a specific plan to use me for His glory, and that I will spend eternity with Him.

You're worth all of that too. As His child, you're worth more than gold, more than diamonds, more than any *thing*. We are worth the eventual healing of all our broken pieces; we'll be so very beautiful when He's finished restoring them… yet we won't be worth more at that point than we already are now.

God made the ultimate sacrifice to save us from spiritual death and everlasting separation from Him. He has plans for you—He didn't rescue us to abandon us. When we're feeling worthless, of no use to anyone, we'll do well to remember: God has proclaimed that we are worth the highest price ever paid.

Forgiven

*As far as the east is from the west, so far hath
he removed our transgressions from us.*
—Psalm 103:12

*We have redemption through his
blood, the forgiveness of sins, according
to the riches of his grace.*
—Ephesians 1:7

Sometimes I feel weighed down by sin, to my very soul. I worry that my failures can never truly be cleansed from me. Things I'm not proud of that I've done in the past can seem as if they are still here, as if they still have a hold on me.

Why is it that we can't forget our sins? I think this is because, so often, we forget that God has.

When we repent of what we've done, God removes that sin from us for eternity, "as far as the east is from the west." Amazingly, not only does He forgive us, He also never again considers the sin or brings it up against us. When we repent, our sin is covered by the righteousness of His Son, and it stays that way.

It is hard to forgive ourselves, yet when we fail to do so, we act as though Christ's blood is not enough to purify us. It is God's judgment alone that counts, and so, once He has forgiven us, we likewise must forgive ourselves, remembering when God looks at us, He doesn't see our sins—He sees our Savior.

Useful

We are his workmanship, created in Christ Jesus unto good works, which God hath before ordained that we should walk in them.
—EPHESIANS 2:10

MANY TIMES I wonder what God could want with me. I'm such a work in progress. How can others see Him in and through me when I commit so many wrongs?

The straight answer is that the Lord uses flawed people for His glory. We see it plainly in His Word: we don't have to be perfect beforehand.

Look at Paul. He had sinned grievously, setting himself up publicly as Christ's enemy, persecuting and killing believers. Yet God used him to spread the good news to so many people in his own day and into the future through his writings.

God saw Paul's potential despite all his faults. He saw, not what Paul was, but what he could be.

In the same way, God sees what He can do through us, and He gives us what we need to accomplish His plans. He can use us to do so much in this world. He can use our testimony and our experiences to touch others who are in pain and don't know the Savior.

Always remember that whoever you are, wherever you are, God will use you for His glory, if you will only let Him.

Understood

*"Who can hide in secret places so that
I cannot see them?" declares the Lord.
"Do I not fill heaven and earth?"*
—Jeremiah 23:24 (NIV)

*The Word was made flesh, and dwelt among us,
and we beheld his glory, the glory as of the only
begotten of the Father, full of grace and truth.*
—John 1:14

There are times when I feel as if no one can really understand what I'm going through. Times when I'm low, and deeply discouraged, and feeling trapped alone in the dark. Times when I deal with temptations and trials I actually feel no one else could have possibly faced before.

This is far from the truth, of course. Through experiences like these, God has reminded me of great difficulties Jesus endured, such as when He was tempted by the devil in the desert, and when, knowing He was soon to face death, he felt utterly alone in the Garden of Gethsemane.

Jesus understands more than we will ever know, for not only is He God, He also is man. This means

He went through everything we undergo. Think about that. Jesus was *here*, among His people! He faced grief, joy, temptation, weariness, peace, pain, comfort, fear … all of what's common to human experience.

God didn't just create us. He is us! I can't get over how miraculous that is. Nothing can compare. He cares so much that He came to earth in human form so He could walk in our shoes, live among us, and then *die* for us. Not only is He all-powerful, He knows what it is to have surrendered all power.

Remember this, the next time you feel alone. There is not one single thing about us, not one facet of humanness, that God doesn't know and understand. He isn't only a King who rules from afar, He came down among us, and He left His Spirit behind to stay. He knows you, He understands you, because He chose to become like you.

Made with a Purpose

*I know the thoughts that I think toward
you, saith the Lord, thoughts of peace, and
not of evil, to give you an expected end.*
—JEREMIAH 29:11

*We know that all things work together for
good to them that love God, to them who
are the called according to his purpose.*
—ROMANS 8:28

BEING FRESH OUT of college, I'm still trying to figure out what God wants me to do with my life. It's a little scary for me. At times I question my purpose, wondering what He wants of me. I'm not fully sure what career path to take, or whether marriage and children are part of His plan for me.

What keeps me going is remembering what God has said in His Word. He knows His plans for me. I may not know what the future holds at the moment, but He sees the full picture. He has the map, and all He asks is that we seek him, listening and watching for His direction.

He has plans for each of us, and we can trust that, no matter where we are in life. I think finding His purpose is an exciting journey. He reveals His will in our lives bit by bit. It's thrilling, finding out His plans even as we're imagining what will come next.

It is, in a way, like a treasure hunt. Think about this, the next time you question your purpose. Rest in the assurance that He has a marvelous journey in store for you.

Gifted for His Glory

*Each of you should use whatever gift you have
received to serve others, as faithful stewards
of God's grace in its various forms.*
—1 PETER 4:10 (NIV)

*There are different kinds of gifts, but the same
Spirit distributes them. There are different
kinds of service, but the same Lord. There are
different kinds of working, but in all of them
and in everyone it is the same God at work.*
—1 CORINTHIANS 12:4–6 (NIV)

EVER SINCE ELEMENTARY school, I have loved to write. I've spent hours and hours over the years filling journals with poetry and stories. I believe that God gave me the ability to write, and He allows me to use this gift to share Him with others.

Everywhere I've been, I have met people with beautiful gifts that they too have received to glorify God. Some people can sing and others paint. Some people are good at sports, or carpentry, or construction, and so on. God gives us all special talents to use for His honor.

But these are not even the most wonderful gifts

He gives us—those are called "spiritual gifts." These can be abilities such as teaching, leadership, encouragement, giving, or preaching. When we place our faith in Jesus, He gives us a spiritual gift, chosen specifically for us; through this, His Spirit can use us to touch others. These gifts are an extraordinary means by which others can see Jesus through us.

Isn't it phenomenal that He chose to empower us in this way? This is God choosing to use us to share His great love! If you haven't found your spiritual gift yet, ask Him today to help you discover it and to begin using it for His glory.

3

LIVING FOR GOD

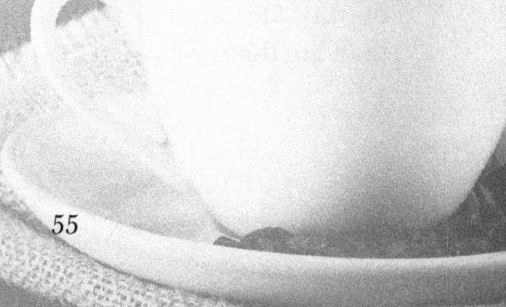

Letting Go of "Me"

*When he had called the people unto him
with his disciples also, he said unto them,
Whosoever will come after me, let him deny
himself, and take up his cross, and follow me.*
—MARK 8:34

IF THERE IS one thing I know about myself, it's that I sometimes struggle with selfishness. Many times I want to do what is pleasing to me, regardless of the effect it has on others and whether or not it's pleasing to Christ. It's hard to let go of selfishness, of sinful things. It's hard to let go of *me*.

However, God says that to truly follow Him, we have to die to our worldly selves. This means that our sinful nature—anything in us that rebels against God, that puts our desires above His—must be completely destroyed. We must put to death any desire that goes against His will for us.

Think of this as sacrificing the "old self" on an altar to the Lord. Incredibly, it's an exchange of our life for an even better one—His! God tells us that when we do this, He can make us into something even better than anything we could possibly have imagined.

If we fail to surrender everything, however, we block God from working in our lives. We cannot be made new while clinging to the old.

If you are holding on to something, to anything that you haven't yet relinquished to God, ask Him to help you to give yourself to Him completely. When we give ourselves up for Him, He will make us into so much more than we could be on our own.

He Is Enough

*My God shall supply all your need according
to his riches in glory by Christ Jesus.*
—PHILIPPIANS 4:19

THERE ARE TIMES that I feel I care too much about material things. I can find I'm too focused on having the nicest clothes, or getting the latest technology. Recently, when I was listening to the song "Everything" by Unspoken, a lyric jumped out at me, with this message: If I have God's love, and nothing else, I already have it all.

And it's true. No matter what happens, no matter what else we have or don't have, as long as we have God's love, we have everything we need. In Him and through Him we have peace, security, comfort, strength, joy, fellowship with other believers and so much more.

God is literally the One who gave us and continues to give us life. Because He sent his Son to die for us, we can be re-made, whole. Through Him we have the assurance that in the end all will be well, and we will be with Him for eternity.

Even if we're starving, suffering in sickness, or

on the cusp of death, as Christians we can know He is always with us, and nothing can take away that certainty. The world can toss us around, but it can never damage our souls. Because of what Jesus did on the cross, our souls have been secured, and even death can't destroy us.

It makes no difference what we have, materially. Our true sustenance is in and through God. He *is* our "everything."

Grounded in His Word

Thy word have I hid in mine heart,
that I might not sin against thee.
—PSALM 119:11

He answered and said, It is written, Man
shall not live by bread alone, but by every word
that proceedeth out of the mouth of God.
—MATTHEW 4:4

WHEN I AM discouraged or down, God often shows me just what I need to see in a verse or devotion. His Word always gives me strength. It gives me joy. I know I could not go through life without being grounded in His Word.

God is our foundation; He keeps us standing. And His Word has wisdom for everything we will ever face. There is no guidebook or instruction manual that could help us more.

Not only that, His Word is filled with His promises. He promises to protect us, to guide us, to carry us through each valley, and so much more. Relying on God's Word, we become armed to fight the evils of this world.

His Word is more valuable than anything we

could imagine. Whatever we go through, whomever and wherever we are, the Holy Spirit can speak to us in any situation through His Word recorded especially for us. When we build our lives around it, nothing in all creation can keep us down.

Look to Him

*Because of his strength will I wait
upon thee: for God is my defence.*
—Psalm 59:9

*Trust in the Lord with all thine heart; and
lean not unto thine own understanding.*
—Proverbs 3:5

$\mathscr{L}$ISTENING TO THE sermon Sunday, something the preacher said really hit me: Too often we try to fight battles that are not ours to fight in the first place.

I tend to do this a lot. A worry won't leave me alone, and I obsess over how to make it go away. Or a temptation looms and I insist on trying to defeat it with my own strength. In doing this, all I'm seeing is what *I* can or can't do in the situation and what *I* should try to do next. The entire time, God's right there with a better solution, but my problems seem so big that I don't bother to look to Him. I don't want to look away from the trouble, and it keeps me from seeing Him.

We all face this. The question is, how do we turn our eyes to God and focus on what He can do? We have to stop staring at our human weaknesses and instead look to His divine power. When we're criticizing our limited abilities and anguishing over how we can possibly cope, *He* is saying, "You don't have to do any of this on your own!"

Read His promises to you until they are embedded in your heart. Concentrate on His great love and might. We will truly see God when we fully realize it's not about what we can do—it's about what He can do, and will do, if we look at and listen to Him instead of ourselves.

True Repentance

Produce fruit in keeping with repentance.
—MATTHEW 3:8 (NIV)

Repent, then, and turn to God, so that your sins may be wiped out, that times of refreshing may come from the Lord.
—ACTS 3:19 (NIV)

MANY, MANY ARE the times I've gone to God asking His forgiveness for a sin I have committed. And far too many are the times I've ended up turning right back around and rushing into that same sin again. All this does is leave me wracked with guilt.

The truth is that true repentance is really and truly difficult. It involves something much deeper than admitting, "Yes, I did that, sorry."

Our English word *repentance* is translated from a Greek term that means "to change one's mind." For most of us, this is an ongoing process, a making of the right decision over and over and over until it has become natural, habitual. The apostle Paul exhorts us to be changed (or transformed) by our mind's renewal; this isn't merely a one-time choice but rather is committing, over the course of a lifetime, to follow God's will in place of our old sinful will.

True repentance is life-changing. It involves our confession that God is God, and we are not; it involves our submitting to His Spirit's reign in our hearts, over any and all sinful inclinations. It's based on asking God to help us turn our heart toward Him and away from sin. As He does, and as our heart does, we'll come to hate sin and love Him, more and more for as many times, and for as long as it takes, until we have become entirely like Jesus.

Are you tired of regrets? If like me you have trouble with true repentance, ask God for His help. Ask Him to help you turn your eyes away from the world and fix them fully on Him. Ask Him for the steadfast strength to keep turning to Him, submitting to His Spirit, and learning to walk in His will. No one who's ever continued making this choice has ever regretted it.

It Starts with a Spark

*As newborn babes, desire the sincere milk
of the word, that ye may grow thereby.*
—1 Peter 2:2

I'VE ALWAYS LOVED sitting by the fire in the winter. It's so cozy. But to get that fire, I can't just pile up some logs and light a match.

Most fires—especially those that are helpful, rather than harmful—start slowly. First you put in kindling, like dry twigs and leaves. Gradually you add larger logs, as small flickers progress all the way to a big blaze.

I find that it's the same way with being on fire for Christ. We tend to want to be enflamed for Him instantly and completely, embarking on and staying immersed in life-changing projects. But, like fire, we aren't designed that way. Fire has to progressively grow, and so do we.

We start by doing "little" things: seeking and following God, loving and caring for others. As we grow in Christ and get to know Him more, His Spirit's fire in us will grow. He will show us where to go from there.

God has never said all our growth—all our becoming—is to happen at once. He can and will do amazing things with our lives, as we live for Him step by step. We have to remember that, like fire, it all begins with a spark.

We Will Hear When We Listen

Be still, and know that I am God; I will be exalted among the heathen, I will be exalted in the earth.
—Psalm 46:10

In all thy ways acknowledge him, and he shall direct thy paths.
—Proverbs 3:6

I AM A BIG user of technology. I love to play around on my phone or laptop, browsing the internet and playing games.

Sometimes, though, this can get in the way of time with God. The world is constantly shouting, howling that we *have to* try this or *must hurry* to do that. The constant stream of new things can become ceaseless distractions that end up consuming our time. We forget about simply being in the quiet, alone with God.

Worldly activities can keep us from growing in Him, giving Him our all, and receiving His blessings, if we allow them to. It is crucial that we stop what we're doing and listen for God's voice. We need to set aside the competition, sit down, and listen to what He has to say in His Word. All the time as the world is shouting at us, He's whispering: "Listen, I have something so important to tell you."

How astounding it is that the Creator of the universe wants to speak to us! He longs to share with us His guidance and love. Every day we should make time to read and reflect on His Word. What He has to say will change us for the better.

Just Speak

> *Confess your faults one to another, and pray one for another, that ye may be healed. The effectual fervent prayer of a righteous man availeth much.*
> –JAMES 5:16

> *Pray without ceasing.*
> –1 THESSALONIANS 5:17

SOMETIMES PRAYER FEELS meaningless. It's like I'm simply saying words, without purpose. My heart, not fully in it, seems anywhere but "here."

In truth, there isn't anything that always *feels* authentic. What's needed is to stop worrying about sounding perfect, focus my whole heart on God, and just speak. It's not about having any ideal "formula" or finding the "right" words. Prayer is interacting with God as we would a friend—someone we care about and who cares for us, someone we want to share with and hear from, and grow nearer to.

Prayer isn't some religious ritual; it's a conversation. God wants us to speak to Him from our hearts, to come to Him with our problems and our praise. When we pray we may be talking to our King, but we're also talking to our best friend;

He wants to comfort us and ease our burdens. We can talk to Him about everything: our sadness, our happiness, *anything,* whether big or small, and He will listen.

When we pray, we are conversing one on one with God. If we do this continually, He will answer in ways better than we can possibly imagine.

"Your Will Be Done"

Teach me to do thy will; for thou art my God: thy spirit is good; lead me into the land of uprightness.
—Psalm 143:10

Abba, Father, all things are possible unto thee; take away this cup from me: nevertheless not what I will, but what thou wilt.
—Mark 14:36

Right now I am in the midst of something many people have experienced at some point: waiting for a callback about a job interview. I wonder whether I'm qualified and capable. Part of me is excited about the possibility of getting the position, and the other part feels like it will be a weight off my shoulders if I don't.

Either way I know, however, that the best thing I can do is lean on God and ask for His will to be done, not mine. The truth is, while sometimes I want what God wants, often I'm more interested in something else. We may think we'll be safer and happier doing whatever we want to do, but throughout my life I have found that embracing God's will is what brings joy and contentment.

Following His will makes us so much more fulfilled than anything else!

When we submit to God, our lives are filled with meaning because we're living for His glory. When we live according to His will, we are no longer striving to make ourselves happy. Instead we're serving Him, helping to fulfill His plans, as we're loving and caring for others.

Living for the One who's given us life in the first place—that's what completes us.

Ever Thankful

O give thanks unto the Lord; for he is good: for his mercy endureth for ever.
—Psalm 136:1

I will praise thee, O Lord, with my whole heart; I will shew forth all thy marvelous works. I will be glad and rejoice in thee: I will sing praise to thy name, O thou most High.
—Psalm 9:1–2

I don't think I'll ever truly comprehend how blessed I am. Among countless other things, I have a family who loves me, food on the table, and, most of all, a God who loves me more than anything. How could I ever show Him just how thankful I am?

We can never give back to God as much as He gives us. Fortunately, He doesn't want flashy or elaborate gifts. All He asks for is our hearts.

Don't get me wrong—I know this can be a hard thing to give. It means surrendering our will to His and choosing to place our life in His hands. That's the very essence of faith.

What we need to remember is that giving

ourselves to God isn't about big rituals. It's step-by-step, day-by-day, *living for Him*.

We tithe, we pray, we read and meditate on His Word, we worship and praise Him, and we try to do what we know to be right—to honor Him with our words and our actions. It's the "little," everyday things like these that show Him just how thankful we are. We give our thanks by serving Him.

Think about it: at the core of all this is our love for Him, which is exactly what He desires. He loved us first; we love Him in return, and this is the kind of thanks that delights His heart.

There Is No Compromise

*No one can serve two masters. Either you will
hate the one and love the other, or you will
be devoted to the one, and despise the other.
You cannot serve both God and money.*
—MATTHEW 6:24 (NIV)

IT IS NOT always easy to follow God. I don't always feel like making the right or best choice. There are times I want to indulge in the world, and the temptation can look so attractive and easy to justify. I tell myself, "It's not so bad," and "I'm not hurting anyone." It makes me feel like I'm a part of the group.

I'm not unique in this. We all want to fit in. We don't want people to think we're different in a negative way.

The simple truth, though, is that we *are* different—and the more like Jesus we become, the less we will conform to the world's standards. We can save ourselves so much anguish by making peace with this fact and embracing it. Then we can keep walking forward in Christ.

Among everything that He perfectly modeled for

us, refusal to compromise always stands out. When religious leaders accused and threatened Him, Jesus didn't back down. He held His ground because He knew He was doing God's will. He stood firm for truth and did so in love.

Jesus wasn't just facing ridicule or outsider status. He faced torture; He faced the cross. Yet He was willing and faithful, for His Father and for us. He could have stayed silent, but He kept doing what He knew was right, no matter what it would cost Him.

God sacrificed His beloved Son for us; sacrificing popular opinion is the least we can do. To follow Christ is to be all in. There is no "halfway"—we're always moving in either one direction or the other.

If we truly love Him, we are truly His disciples, and that means following Him wherever He leads. The One who gave His own life to save us will not compromise His love for us. In turn, we endeavor to live completely for Him.

Designed to Thrive

Just as you received Christ Jesus as Lord, continue to live your lives in him, rooted and built up in him, strengthened in the faith as you were taught, and overflowing with thankfulness.
—COLOSSIANS 2:6–7 (NIV)

I DON'T LIKE TO admit it, but many times I choose the easy path. I coast along, not stepping up to challenges or digging deeper in my faith. I'll find that I have *settled*, not only in general but specifically in my relationship with God. That I've become okay with going through motions, getting by on some notion of the bare minimum.

In truth, I don't ever want to become an "okay Christian"; I want to become the best me I can possibly be. God didn't create us for mediocrity, but anytime we settle, that's where we're heading. We are not letting Him transform our lives to the fullest.

This isn't to say we can't take time to enjoy the growth that God has brought about in us. It also doesn't mean we have to overcommit and wear ourselves out. However, in our walk with Jesus, in this life, we don't reach perfection. Whenever we believe we've reached a point beyond which there's no more growth, or no more need for growth, in any area, we're being misled.

There is so much God wants to teach us and show us. When we settle, we are becoming okay with less than the best He has to offer. God wants us to get out of our comfort zone, face new challenges, and grow in our understanding of His Word. In this way not only will we grow in Him, we will thrive.

Ask Him to open your heart, your mind, your eyes, your ears. Every new day brings something new to do or to learn. We can't just stand still. We have to chase after Him, and as we do we will become stronger, wiser, and a little more like Him every day.

Reset

> *Rid yourselves of all the offenses you have committed, and get a new heart and a new spirit.... I will cleanse you from all your impurities and from all your idols.... I will remove from you your heart of stone and give you a heart of flesh.*
> —Ezekiel 18:31; 36:25–26 (niv)

> *Create in me a pure heart, O God, and renew a steadfast spirit within me.*
> —Psalm 51:10 (niv)

As a writer, sometimes I struggle to come up with something I think will be worth sharing. I go through a lot of drafts! That's one good thing about writing: If something goes off track, I can always start over.

Do you know, in a way, that we can also do this with our lives? When we first give ourselves to Christ, He resets us, making us new and placing His Spirit within us to be our guide. From then on, the living God is alive in us and helping us to live our lives for Him.

Of course, having a human nature, we aren't going

to follow Him perfectly. We're still going to mess up. Giving ourselves to God and placing ourselves in His hands doesn't make us perfect. But it does begin the process of perfecting us—of making us more like Him with every choice that we make to live for Him. And that's where it just keeps getting better. When we repent of our wrongdoing (sin), He cleanses and restores (in a sense, resets) us once again.

If you're like me, there will be a lot of times when you need a reset. Whether you have drifted from Him, or allowed a habitual sin to return, or stumbled in a different way, it doesn't matter. Jesus promises that when we come to Him in true repentance—when we confess, ask forgiveness for, and turn from our sin—He will cleanse and refresh us, renewing our hearts for Him.

If presently there is anything in you that stands between you and the God who saved you and loves you, pray for a reset. Ask Him to renew your heart. Wherever you are, whatever you've done, it's never too late.

4

IN THE VALLEYS

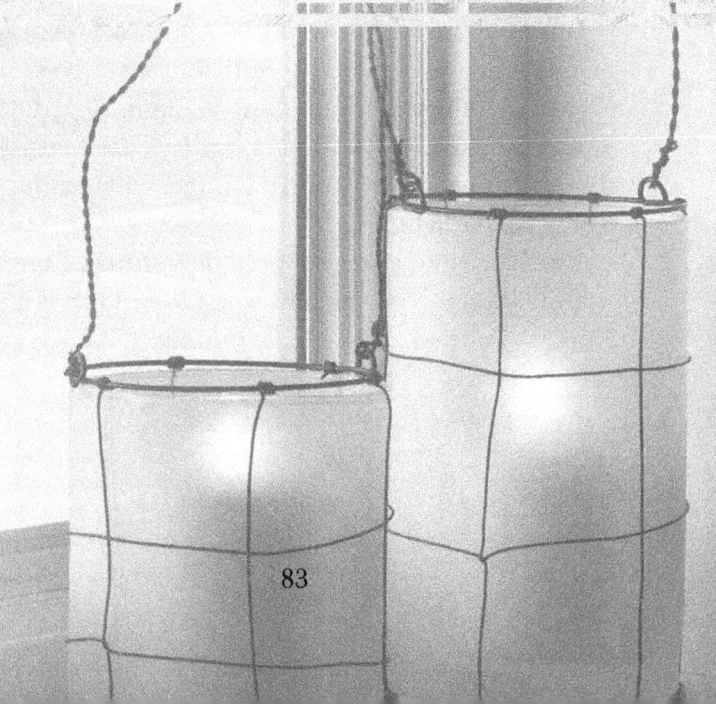

Fighting the Good Fight

Be strong in the Lord and in his mighty power.
—Ephesians 6:10 (NIV)

*Fight the good fight of the faith. Take
hold of the eternal life to which you were
called when you made your good confession
in the presence of many witnesses.*
—1 Timothy 6:12 (NIV)

As we journey through life, we come across mountaintops, places of happiness. We feel confident, as if nothing can shake us. Everything seems as it should be.

But as happy as those special times may be, every one of us, at some point, will find ourselves on a downward slope into a valley. It might be gradual; it may be like a quick tumble. Valleys are filled with disappointments, with sorrows, and with battles we feel we can't fight.

I've had quite a few of these downturns. I tend to try to fight my way out, and when I do, I just fall flat. I end up curled into a ball, thinking, Woe is me—there's no way I can do this.

When I have this attitude, though, I'm overlooking

something very important. God is stronger than any opponent, with more than enough strength for any battle I may face. He always has what we need; if we're willing to humble ourselves, leaning on Him and asking for His direction, we will find it.

God also gives us himself—we can listen to and speak directly with Him. He will grant us wisdom and the strength of His Word, the help of friends and family, and the ability to walk whatever path lies ahead. In the valley, we may feel like there's no way we can triumph, but through Him we *can*.

When life has you down, never give up. Instead of wasting time and energy on self-pity, look up. Get up, put on His armor, and stand your ground. Nothing can tear down what God lifts up.

Praise Him in the Storm

Consider it pure joy, my brothers and sisters, whenever you face trials of many kinds; because you know that the testing of your faith produces perseverance.
—James 1:2–3 (NIV)

I HAVE BEEN THROUGH many valleys: depression, hospital stays, dealing with disabilities, and more. There have been many times when I wondered why God would let me go through so much pain. Depression, in particular, has brought many storms, making me wonder what God's purpose in it could possibly be.

What I've learned is that, through severe trials, I grow in faith; in love; in Him. Without the pain, I wouldn't know what it is to receive His comfort. I wouldn't know how wonderful it is to be utterly enveloped in His joy. I wouldn't seek, or find, the peace that can't come from anywhere else.

It's in weakness and in struggle that I run to Him, and He draws me nearer. Suffering is what turns us toward Him, so it's through suffering that we come to know Him, and become more like Him.

We come to realize that rather than going to Him only in our darkest times, we need Him and belong with Him *all* the time.

This is why, as the Casting Crowns song is titled, I will "Praise You in This Storm," valleys are necessary; God uses them to refine us, to strengthen our faith and bring us closer to Him. If we're willing, it's through trials and challenges that we will most clearly see His power and experience His love.

There's no easy road that provides a greater blessing than the way we experience God through hardship. Instead of focusing on our difficulties, instead of obsessing over how to extricate ourselves from suffering, let's turn our hearts, minds, and eyes to the One who has given us life—and praise Him for the good He does even in our darkest times.

Spirit Versus Flesh

No temptation has overtaken you except what is common to mankind. And God is faithful; he will not let you be tempted beyond what you can bear. But when you are tempted, he will also provide a way out so that you can endure it.
—1 Corinthians 10:13 (NIV)

Submit yourselves therefore to God. Resist the devil, and he will flee from you.
—James 4:7

LIKE EVERYONE, I face temptations, my own personal monsters. And, unfortunately, on the outside they don't look like monsters—they look beautiful. They also don't tell the truth upfront; rather, they smoothly pledge to be fulfilling, to grant me all that I supposedly lack.

I have found out, the hard way, that however they look, and whatever they say, they're poison. They infect everything they touch. Any momentary sense of "fulfillment" is replaced quickly with guilt and shame. You know why it's so hard for me to battle them? It's because while the spirit sees them for what they are, the flesh is weak and easily tricked.

Paul the apostle says we all face this ongoing battle between flesh and spirit. On our own, we aren't strong. This is why we submit to and lean on God. He's told us himself: if we do, He will show us a way out.

Think of a temptation as an alluring door. No matter how convinced we are that something fabulous is behind it, it only conceals a disaster in the making. God knows what's back there; He warns us to turn away from that door, and then He points us to a better one. Yes, it's tough to listen and obey (it looks *so* enticing). But remember: when God wills something different from what we think we want, His way is always–*always*–ultimately more satisfying.

God designed us; we were made to be fueled by Him. That's why His way for us is the only path to fulfillment. Gratification from sin lasts moments. Nothing parallels true joy and contentment, and these are found in what honors God.

The "Perfect" Exchange

*I, even I, am he who blots out your
transgressions, for my own sake, and
remembers your sins no more.*
—Isaiah 43:25 (NIV)

When I face temptations, I give in more often than I'd like to admit. When I trip and fall, I feel covered in mud, as if there's grime deep in my skin and I'll never get clean. I ask myself how I can possibly be a follower of Christ if I'm so prone to failure.

This is exactly what the devil wants, for us to obsess over the guilt we feel, instead of bringing our offenses to the Lord in repentance. He doesn't want us to experience forgiveness; he wants us to become paralyzed with shame and to convince us that "this time you've done it for good—there's no way back now."

That's not how God works. As the adage goes, "Satan says: look at your sin. God says: look at My Son" (anonymous). We can never be good enough and we don't have to be. We only need to accept His grace. The blood of Jesus covers our sins, and even though we are sinners, His righteousness makes us forgiven and loved, always.

God wants us to be perfect, but the "perfection" He asks of us isn't ours—it's His! His Spirit, alive in us, is what gives us the ability to do as He directs. Beating ourselves up when we err isn't godly; it's prideful, self-focused. If we fail, we repent of (turn away from) the sin, confessing our wrong and receiving His forgiveness.

We are only human. And God only requires of us what we are able to give. That's our old sinful nature, for which He gives us himself! He calls us to obey His Spirit, living in and through us, instead of our "only human" self. From there, we rely on Him, and He handles the rest.

Living Fearlessly

Fear thou not; for I am with thee: be not dismayed; for I am thy God: I will strengthen thee; yea, I will help thee; yea, I will uphold thee with the right hand of my righteousness.
—Isaiah 41:10

God hath not given us the spirit of fear; but of power, and of love, and of a sound mind.
—2 Timothy 1:7

When I was going through my deepest bout of depression, I was terrified. I didn't know what would happen next. I had no idea how I could overcome it. I was desperately fearful that the experience would become even worse.

Thank God, there was at least one thing I got right: in the crushing vise-grip of that situation, I managed to remember to rely on Him, to let Him lead. No matter how consuming fear may feel, it cannot conquer us when we trust the Lord. He is the almighty—*all-mighty*—God; in the face of anxiety, and doubt, and panic, His Spirit will bolster us with power, with love, and with soundness of mind.

Think about that. His love is greater than any

fear. He *will* strengthen us and hold us up. And He never abandons us to confront enemies alone.

Always know that if you are a child of God, you are shielded by His love. His love envelops you, every moment—in every moment when you feel it, and in every moment when you don't. Because no fear can overcome that love, we can live fearlessly in Him.

Cast Away Worries

*Cast all your anxiety on him
because he cares for you.*
—1 Peter 5:7 (NIV)

*Take no thought, saying, What shall we eat? or,
What shall we drink? or, Wherewithal shall we
be clothed? For your heavenly Father knoweth
that ye have need of all these things. But seek ye
first the kingdom of God, and his righteousness;
and all these things shall be added unto you.*
—Matthew 6:31–33

During my last year of graduate school, I was inundated with worry about comprehensive finals. As the word implies, this test would cover everything I'd learned. I had to pass it to graduate … and I just knew I was going to flunk.

We all have faced worries. They can eat away at us whether they're about smaller things (maybe a school exam), or bigger (maybe biopsy results). Another thing most of us have in common? Finding it hard to bring them to God and trust in Him for whatever answers and help we need.

The wisdom and guidance that Jesus directed

toward our worries is based around two corresponding themes. First, fretting is futile—it doesn't accomplish anything, so we shouldn't waste time and energy on it. And second, the Lord has the resources for resolving our challenges, so we should focus on Him and not ourselves. His Word is filled with stories of His endless care and gracious provision for people just like us.

Our God is a big God. When we get carried away with worries, we insinuate that our problems are bigger. In truth, we worship and serve a God capable of handling *anything* we may face. Because of this, we can cast our cares upon Him and let them stay there.

Dismissing Doubt

When you ask [God for wisdom], you must believe and not doubt, because the one who doubts is like a wave of the sea, blown and tossed by the wind.
—James 1:6 (NIV)

"Truly I tell you, if you have faith and do not doubt ... you can say to this mountain, 'Go, throw yourself into the sea,' and it will be done."
—Matthew 21:21 (NIV)

Sometimes it's hard to hear what my heart is telling me over what the devil is shouting. He uses anything he can to introduce doubt. Hesitations accumulate and pile up, making me feel frozen in my tracks, keeping me from walking even one more step toward becoming who God designed me to be.

Doubt can be overwhelming, especially in life's times of uncertainty. If granted enough power, it can cause us to have misgivings about virtually anything. Satan fosters doubt because he knows that if we entertain it, our faith shrinks while fear takes God's place in our hearts.

As humans we know we'll all face doubts from time to time—so what can we do about this? We start with listening to and believing God. His Word is filled with His promises and assurances for us. He tells us we're His children; He guarantees that everything is in His hands; He reminds that through Him all things are possible.

We belong to the Creator, the King. He says one thing, while the world says another. We choose whom to believe.

Then, we also remember and look at what God has already done in our lives. He has loved us, saved us, helped us, blessed us more times and in more ways than we even know—we can reflect on and cling to what we do know. It strengthens faith to bring to mind what He has done ... and to know that He hasn't changed a bit since the last time we saw Him at work. Nor will He change. Ever.

When the devil says, "God cannot help you," we say, "See how He's helped already." And as our faith grows stronger and deeper, doubts fade like the dust they truly are.

Crushing the Night

*This is the message we have heard from
him and declare to you: God is light;
in him there is no darkness at all.*
—1 JOHN 1:5 (NIV)

*The Lord is close to the brokenhearted; he
rescues those whose spirits are crushed.*
—PSALM 34:18 (NLT)

FOR A LONG time now I've been living with a monster inside. I experience this black beast, depression, as a darkness that feels unshakable, a darkness millions of others likewise know all too well. Its voice reminds, again and again, of all the mistakes you've made; it says you're worthless ... pointless ... hopeless. Sometimes it brings sadness. Other times it just leaves me numb.

Even so, every time I've fought this fiend, I've always known deep down that God is with me. Sometimes it's hard to feel Him there—sometimes I *feel* entirely alone—but I know the truth all the same. The truth is, darkness doesn't stand a chance against God.

God is light; because He's given me His Spirit, light never leaves me, no matter what my eyes see, or think they see. If you've encountered extreme physical darkness, you've probably also seen how even a bit of light creates a stark difference. The source of light itself doesn't merely encroach upon darkness: Light crushes the night.

Thinking on this, some time ago, inspired me to write a poem about my experiences:

I Will Stand

I'm Bending
But just see if I'll break
If you think you own me that's your
    mistake
Because I am strong
And God's been with me long before you
    came

You sneak
And you claw your way in
Look at me with your Cheshire grin
But God is stronger than anything you'll
    throw my way
All the stuff you say, telling me I'm less than

Telling me I'm flawed, broken, not worth
    the breath in my lungs
But that's God's breath He gave me
And when He made me He said, "You are
    loved"

When you toss your words like weapons,
    He tosses back

Loved, priceless, covered with His blood
He covered my life in a changing flood
Looked at me saying, "My Son makes you
    worthy"
And you dare say I'm nothing?
I am a child of the King

Oh, there'll be days when you creep up
But I know when times get rough He's there
And I'll carry on with my Jesus' light
Cause the smallest bit can crush the night
So you ... will ... fail

So run off with your tail between your legs
Back to the dregs of filth from whence you
    came
Cause I can tell you in Jesus' name
You will crumble, I will not stumble
On His rock I will stand

The darkness around us cannot conquer the light within us. If we have God's light, there's nowhere for evil to hide–there, its pretense is revealed for what it is. He is bigger and stronger than anything that attacks. Remain in the light, and you *will* triumph.

In the Valleys

Constant in the Change

> *"Though the mountains be shaken and the hills be removed, yet my unfailing love for you will not be shaken nor my covenant of peace be removed," says the Lord, who has compassion on you.*
> —Isaiah 54:10 (NIV)

> *Heaven and earth shall pass away, but my words shall not pass away.*
> —Matthew 24:35

> *Jesus Christ is the same yesterday and today and forever.*
> —Hebrews 13:8 (NIV)

While it seems there are few people for whom dealing with change comes naturally, I have particular difficulty navigating and accepting it. Because I've been diagnosed as being on the autism spectrum, change has been something that intensely frightens me. I have found I need structure and routine.

I faced one big change when I was fourteen. My mom and dad felt God was calling us to a new church home. I was horrified. I did not want to move away from the church family I loved.

My family had belonged to the same church for

generations. I was going to miss my pastor; I'd miss the women who had taught me about God since I was a little girl. Even worse was that my grandparents wouldn't be moving with us. I had sat with them every Sunday I could remember.

Even so, there were factors that would make this change a good thing. The Lord would lead us to a new church, and as time passed, I found that He had a purpose for us there. I would give my life to Jesus there, and then grow close to God. And I'd meet fellow believers who would walk alongside me through what would prove to be some of the greatest obstacles I had yet faced.

There were two main lessons the experience taught me. First, though change may be scary, we can rest assured that God has reasons for bringing it into our lives. It isn't random or pointless—if we allow it, He will use the effects of change to strengthen and sharpen us.

Second, though we face change, God remains constant. He has never changed and never will—He's the same now and forever. There's nothing we might encounter that He doesn't understand completely, so we can always lean on Him for help.

That's simply extraordinary. No matter what change may come our way, God is always the same loving, merciful, powerful God. We can stand on Him with no worry of falling.

Desert Dry

*Ask, and it shall be given you; seek, and ye shall
find; knock, and it shall be opened unto you.*
—Matthew 7:7

*I will give you a new heart and put a new spirit
in you; I will remove from you your heart of
stone and give you a heart of flesh. And I will
put my Spirit in you and move you to follow
my decrees and be careful to keep my laws.*
—Ezekiel 36:26–27 (NIV)

There have been times when I've reached a spiritual desert and it feels like the well of Living Water has gone dry. I'm so thirsty I think I'd give anything for a drink, and yet I can't seem to find a drop.

The thing is, deserts generally don't just pop up by themselves, and they don't come to us. Usually, we've brought ourselves there.

In my case, dire thirst often happens when I've been following God half-heartedly. I want to go His way and mine, but I can't do both. I can't get satisfaction in myself, and He can't give me what I need if I don't follow Him all the way.

That's how I end up parched. From there, the question is how to get out of that place and back to where I belong.

I've learned how to take the first step. God says to rely on Him, not on ourselves. All we have to do is ask for His guidance and advice. He *will* answer.

There is always Living Water for us. We just have to get it His way, not ours.

5

Doing unto Others

Willing to Serve

Very truly I tell you, no servant is greater than his master, nor is a messenger greater than the one who sent him. Now that you know these things, you will be blessed if you do them.
—JOHN 13:16–17 (NIV)

Do nothing out of selfish ambition or vain conceit. Rather, in humility value others above yourselves.
—PHILIPPIANS 2:3 (NIV)

THIS WORLD IS hard on the weak. Getting ahead and staying there doesn't leave room for helping others along. A me-first mindset pushes people down rather than lifting them up.

Sometimes we find ourselves taking on the world's every-man-for-himself mentality. We may chalk up people's needs to their laziness, or cluelessness, and thus absolve ourselves of lending a hand. It's tempting, and easy, to look down on others—to compare their flawed spots with our strong points and so deem ourselves superior.

To the world, giving without expecting something in return is absurd. Being a "servant"? That's what somebody who has nothing does to survive.

We know otherwise. We rise not by proclaiming and elevating ourselves but through humility, through selflessness. The truth is that there's great joy in serving others, and joy is only one of giving's many rewards.

Jesus loved—He *lived*—to serve others. The divine King lowered himself and became a man; the Creator came to serve His creation. He willingly came as a servant to show us God's love, to save us.

In our service, we serve as God's hands, allowing Him to reach others through us. Through us, His servants, He changes hearts and lives. When we choose to serve, God's love and light, mighty to save, can shine into our needy world.

Be Their Voice

*Speak up for those who cannot speak for
themselves, for the rights of all who are destitute.*
—Proverbs 31:8 (NIV)

When I was a little girl, I was diagnosed with learning disabilities that affected my performance in school. I was in no position to advocate for myself. My mother became my voice, fighting for accommodations that would give me a chance to be on equal footing with my classmates.

Over the years I have come to recognize that there are people all around us who need help meeting their needs. People who are physically, emotionally, and/or spiritually disabled. People God loves. Whether they lack influence, or strength, or knowledge, or hope, they need an advocate—a voice.

When we step forward to be a voice for those unable to speak for themselves, they get the chance to see God's hands, and God's heart. They can see Him at work; they can see His love, can realize their value in His eyes. They can come to know that He knows them, and longs for them to know Him.

No matter the need, God can meet it. Often, He

wants to meet it through us. He wants to use us to show others their priceless worth to Him. When we lift our voice to speak for those in need, God's love is heard and seen.

Love Is Greatest

Love your enemies, bless them that curse you, do good to them that hate you, and pray for them which despitefully use you, and persecute you.
—MATTHEW 5:44

And now these three remain: faith, hope and love. But the greatest of these is love.
—1 CORINTHIANS 13:13 (NIV)

IT BREAKS MY heart, the way the world is today. Seemingly there are endless reservoirs of white-hot rage, and ice-cold bitterness. Everything is *them* against *us*. There's so much hate.

We tend to look at those who hate us, who wish to harm us, and want to hurt them back. We close our hearts to love and open them to resentment. We want to see our foes not rescued and saved but crushed and annihilated.

These tactics will not work. We can't fight hate with hate—that just makes the original hatred grow stronger while breeding and fueling more. Evil for evil is the lowest road; that's the world's way, and if we embrace it we reinforce the false idea that Christ's followers are no different than everyone else.

We can only effectively combat hate with love. That's what Jesus called us to do. And, as He said, that's what will show the world we belong to Him—not having great power, not having right answers, not being the happiest people on the planet, but that we love, each other *and* those who hate us.

Love is stronger than hate in every situation. Hate consumes and destroys, but love strengthens and builds. Choosing love isn't easy, and hate won't disappear merely by coming into contact with love, but that's not up to us. We can trust God for the ultimate results. Our obedience opens doors for His love to reach the hearts of others, and from there anything is possible.

A Heart That Forgives

*If you forgive other people when they sin against
you, your heavenly Father will also forgive
you. But if you do not forgive others their
sins, your Father will not forgive your sins.*
—Matthew 6:14–15 (NIV)

When my mom was just seventeen, she lost her best friend: her sister Kathy. She couldn't understand why it happened. And she developed such a hate for the person who'd taken her sister's life.

Decades later, police, with my mom's help, found the man who was guilty of the crime. Of course, the hatred roared to the surface too. Thankfully, she belonged to God; He spoke to her heart, and she knew she had to forgive the man. I will never forget what she did. She wrote to him, a letter of forgiveness, and she sent it to him along with a Bible.

I was never more proud of my mother. And I've never been more grateful for God—I knew she was able to do this only because He lives in her heart. He helped her to see and understand how this man was lost and hurting and, without God, without hope.

There are many reasons we must forgive those

who hurt us. The most important is that God has forgiven us. Without His forgiveness, we would be forever lost—how could we then turn to others and, presuming to stand in His place, deem *them* unworthy? We carried a debt we couldn't possibly have repaid, and God's Son covered it. To refuse forgiveness to another is a slap in His face.

Another reason is what unforgiveness does to us. The Lord saved my mom the fate of being poisoned from the inside out. Her hatred wouldn't have harmed the killer—it would have eaten *her* alive and damaged her relationship with God. Forgiving the one who has wronged us removes a heavy burden from our shoulders.

Also, when we grant forgiveness, we gain a better understanding of what God did for us. It gives us visceral reminders of the price our Savior paid to release us from sin and show us the way back to God. Truly realizing how much we have been forgiven sets us free to forgive others in turn, to show them God's love and shine His light on the path to His forgiveness.

Share the Burden

*Carry each other's burdens, and in this
way you will fulfill the law of Christ.*
—GALATIANS 6:2 (NIV)

MANY YEARS AGO, the daughter of my former pastor was diagnosed with leukemia. Such an illness is a great burden to bear among any family. We, as their church family, knew we were called to help, and that we were able. Many of us went to spend time with her at St. Jude's. We held fund-raisers at the church to assist with finances. We did whatever we could to come alongside them and share the load until, several years later, she was declared cancer free.

As Christians we're instructed to help shoulder each other's challenges. Having someone to aid us in this manner helps us to better navigate whatever difficulties life brings us. When we do this for others, we're also following the Lord's example.

And Jesus didn't just give us an assist with our burden of sin—He took it *all* upon himself, accepting the complete punishment so that we could be made right with God, forgiven. In bearing the burdens of others, we share that perfect love of Christ. When we follow in His steps, we also may find opportunities for guiding others to the even better step of laying down their troubles at the foot of the cross.

Sonnets or Swords?

> *The tongue has the power of life and death;*
> *and those who love it will eat its fruit.*
> —Proverbs 18:21 (NIV)

> *The tongue is a smart part of the body, but*
> *it makes great boasts. Consider what a great*
> *forest is set on fire by a small spark.*
> —James 3:5 (NIV)

I HAVE ALWAYS LOVED words. They're so much fun to play with, and no matter how many we learn there are always more to discover. They have multiple facets, and untold uses. With words we can fashion beauty; we can share thoughts and feelings; we can teach, and be taught; we can record history; we can tell or craft stories, and recite or create poetry. We can spread kindness and encouragement.

However, with words we can also do massive damage. For example, we know well that when someone says something mean or hurtful, their words can slice deeply and stick with us. You can think of painful words aimed at you without pondering too long, right? Even if years, or decades, have passed since they were launched, some of their cuts and craters can still be felt. Word wounds can last a lifetime.

Words have meaning. And words have power—this should humble us, and make us cautious. Often we can't know whether what we say will bounce right off someone or pierce to their core; even if we know what we meant when we said them, our words may not have the intended effect. Further, their impact can be far greater than we wished. What's more, if we're capable of injuring others with words when we meant no such thing, how much more might we damage someone when we *do* mean to harm?

Let us think before we speak, and ask the Lord to search our hearts and reveal to us our motives. If the tongue's power is sufficient so that in His Word He repeatedly warns and chastises us to guard and control it, we dare not take the matter lightly. Let's ask Him to teach us how to keep from using words as whips or knives and instead to lay hold of chances for using them to bless, and delight, and hearten.

Pass It On

The words of the reckless pierce like swords,
but the tongue of the wise brings healing.
—Proverbs 12:18 (NIV)

Encourage one another and build each other up.
—1 Thessalonians 5:11 (NIV)

One day, when my family was at the mall, I was feeling particularly down. Going through a severe bout with depression, feeling beset by an intense sadness, I asked God to send me an angel, and He did.

I ran right into my best friend. Ross and I met senior year of high school, and he's a huge nerd just like me. We can spend hours talking about our favorite books and shows and theorizing about the plots and characters.

That day his friendship was exactly what I needed. Just talking with him made me happier. It was only for a short while, but merely getting to catch up and obsess over the latest movies we'd seen made me feel so much lighter and put a smile on my face.

So many times we interact with people at a bare-minimum level, not pausing to consider, or ask, what they may be feeling or what's going on in their lives. We may not even acknowledge them. That experience at the mall helped me to remember how much of a difference we can make by being kind. Ross was just being my friend, but in doing so he made my day.

It's so easy to become absorbed in our own concerns and priorities. Meanwhile, all around us, right behind us, walking past us, is someone carrying hurt. Someone under the power of fear. Someone enduring grief. Someone lonely and sad. Someone who needs to see and know God's love.

This is why simple kindness is so important. Just a smile, one small gesture of care, of goodwill, could make a difference. Little things sometimes have the biggest impact. And one thing we all have in common, whatever our station, whatever our situation—we all need God's love. We who belong to Him can share it, constantly and generously.

Even The Tiniest Ray

Ye are the light of the world. A city that is set on an hill cannot be hid. Neither do men light a candle, and put it under a bushel, but on a candlestick; and it giveth light unto all that are in the house. Let your light so shine before men, that they may see your good works, and glorify your Father which is in heaven.
—MATTHEW 5:14–16

I am the light of the world. Whoever follows me will never walk in darkness, but will have the light of life.
—JOHN 8:12 (NIV)

I WAS SAVED WHEN I was seventeen, and ever since then I have lived in the light of God. He surrounds me with His Holy Spirit and His Word. Whenever I need encouragement or comfort He speaks to me. During experiences with depression, anxiety, fear, and other trials, He reminds me of His love, whether through Scripture, through others, or through a devotion, a song, or one of many other ways. No matter how He reaches me, His rays of light bring me such peace.

God changed our lives with His light; He wants us to share it with others. He calls us to let it shine out, never to hide or be ashamed of Him. However we share the gospel, whether by word or by deed, it's a ray of light, one that can pierce the darkness in ways we may never know or see.

When we share God's light, we share His love, which, as the greatest power in existence, can do more than we can possibly imagine. It's the light that has brought us out of darkness—let's share it so that through us God may show others how to receive the same.

Be Bold

> *Go into all the world and preach*
> *the gospel to all creation.*
> —MARK 16:15 (NIV)
>
> *Go ye therefore, and teach all nations,*
> *baptizing them in the name of the Father, and*
> *of the Son, and of the Holy Ghost: Teaching*
> *them to observe all things whatsoever I have*
> *commanded you: and, lo, I am with you*
> *always, even unto the end of the world.*
> —MATTHEW 28:19–20

THE BAPTIST COLLEGE Ministry at the university I attended inspired me with some of their projects. Some days I would walk onto campus, and the sidewalks would be covered with verses and other quotes in chalk. On certain days the ministry would offer dollar lunches. One thing that stood out to me personally was when a girl confidently came up to my table as I ate and asked if there was anything she could pray about with me.

The boldness of the school's Christian students inspired me.

God wants us to be bold for Him. He's fully

capable of reaching anyone, anywhere, at any time, yet apart from the wonders of creation He most often reveals himself through His children. He's given us a mission: to make Him known, to tell of His works and share His Word.

Think about this. God made us in His image—that is, as persons. Faith, like life, is relational; He fashioned us to be connected, rather than isolated. That goes a long way in explaining why God desires to use us to reach those who don't yet know Him.

There are people around the world who still have never heard the name of Jesus. But usually we need not go far to find others who aren't connected to Him. God wants them to know Him too. If we step up and share, He may touch their lives just as He has touched ours.

Whatever the world may say, let's ignore it. Whatever our fears and insecurities may convey, let's overcome them, in His strength. Let's be bold: take a stand and step out for Christ. When we do, there's no telling what He may do.

About the Author

Brittany Wilson has had a love for writing from the time she could pick up a pen, which led to a Master's Degree in English from the University of Louisiana at Monroe. She now works as a reporter and editor for her local newspaper. She enjoys reading, writing, singing, and relaxing with her cat, Happy. *Blessed Assurance* is her first book, and she hopes it won't be her last. With a love for God and a zest for life, she wants to use her writing to encourage others.

www.ingramcontent.com/pod-product-compliance
Lightning Source LLC
LaVergne TN
LVHW091308080426
835510LV00007B/417